Gabriela Sabatini
MY STORY

Published by Great American Publications Division, Avatar General Corporation.

Second Printing — March 1995

ISBN No. 1-886612-00-5

Acknowledgments

———————◆❚◆———————

Edited by Paul Feldman.

Book and cover design by Ogdemli/Feldman Design, North Hollywood, CA.

Special thanks to ProServ, Richard P. Dell and Rosana Galvan.

Photos courtesy of Osvaldo and Beatriz Sabatini from family archives.

Front cover photography by Eddie Adams.

Back cover photography by Clive Brunskill.

Back cover photo courtesy of Allsport, Santa Monica, CA.

Gabriela Sabatini • MY STORY

Table of Contents

This book is dedicated to all the young people of the world who are reaching out to learn skills that will motivate them to become anything they want to be. It is my strongest hope that, through my story, young people will discover that they too can learn how to do great things with their own lives. It will teach them that with hard work, discipline, courage and sacrifice in search of a dream, it is possible to become anything they want to be.

1
———◆———

The River Plate Club

The ball was flying across the court so fast that I could hardly see it. Back and forth, back and forth! I was so excited! What was this marvelous game? I tried to keep my eyes on the ball. It was going so fast! I was only six years old then. My father, brother and uncle had taken me to a tennis club called **"The River Plate Club."** This was in my hometown of Buenos Aires, Argentina in South America on that day in 1976 that changed my life forever.

"Daddy," I asked in Spanish because I could only speak Spanish then, "what game is that?"

"It is called tennis, Gaby."

"May I play? Please? It looks like so much fun!" I pleaded.

There were twenty courts and all of them were occupied. Everyone was wearing beautiful white tennis costumes, the women in little tennis dresses with white skirts, the men in shorts. I could feel the energy and excitement of the game, and I loved it. I wanted to do that. I wanted it more than anything! More than riding my bike, more than watching TV, more than even eating chocolate — and that was something! To run and jump and hit the ball over the net! It would be great!

We had to wait for over two hours before a court was available. I kept asking my father, "When will it be our turn? I want to play!"

"Soon Gaby, soon. You must learn to be patient," he answered.

"I'll be patient later, Daddy. I want to play *right now!*"

We finally got a court. My father handed me a racquet. It was so big it was almost bigger than I was. He hit the ball to me from a little distance. I swung, and I hit the ball back to him. I was thrilled! We did that until he was tired, then Osvaldo, my big brother — he was eleven years old then — took over until he was tired. Then it was my uncle's turn. I tired him out too, but I didn't want to stop. The more I played, the more energy I got. I was so proud! I was only six years old and I could almost keep up with people much older and bigger than I was.

After that first visit to the Club, we came back many times. My father, brother, and uncle taught me the rules of tennis and how to hit the ball better. They would first hit the ball to me from a little distance, then the distance became gradually greater. I was able to keep up with them as much as a six-year-old could, running this way and that around the court. I must have looked like a little playful puppy scampering all over the place.

It didn't take long for tennis to take over my whole life. Every day I would wake up thinking about tennis. At night I'd sleep dreaming of tennis. On weekends my family and I would play at the Club. Sometimes they would miss the easy shots and sometimes I would too. And sometimes I would even win over my father or brother! The more I played, the easier the game became, and I was winning more and more! It was nonstop fun all the way!

When my father went to work, he would drop my brother Osvaldo and me off at the Club on the way to the office. There we would practice together. Some days, however, Osvaldo couldn't go. On those days my father would take me to the Club, leave me there, and pick me up later to take me home. At these times, I would watch the other players and sometimes I'd find someone else with whom to play. This was a lot of fun too.

2

My First Racquet

At the Club I always had to play with an old racquet from home. It was a wonderful toy for me, made of wood and special strings. The handle was wrapped in black tape, and was a little frayed or "fuzzy" on the edges. Every day, when I had finished playing with it, I would put it back in my closet or under my bed for safe-keeping.

After many months of this, I said to my father, "It would be so nice to have my own new racquet. Have I been patient enough?"

He smiled, shook my hand, and said "Yes, you have. It's a deal."

The very next day he came home from work with a new wooden racquet. I was crazy about it. It was the perfect size and color, and it was so clean and new! The store had wrapped it like a present. The racquet had that familiar smell of the tennis racquets at the club, but somehow *it smelled newer*. I thanked my father, gave him a big kiss and a hug, and ran outside with my new toy to play. My first test of the new racquet was the patio wall at home. It worked. It was wonderful! This was my own magic racquet with a life and power all its own. And it was all mine!

3

———◗◖———

A World of Walls

By the time I was six and a half, I was playing every day at the Club. Sometimes I would play with my brother, sometimes on weekends or evenings with my parents, and sometimes with other young players. I made a lot of friends at the Club. When the courts weren't available, I would use the walls at the Club. But when it was really busy at the Club, I would have to wait in line even to use a wall.

There were two particular Club walls I liked to play. One wall was very smooth, and very straight. It was the easiest to play, since the balls almost always bounced right back to me. The other wall was a little curved, and this was very hard to play. Every time the ball would hit, it would bounce back at an angle, maybe two or three feet away, and I would have to run faster and harder to reach it. Because this was harder, it was more available for practice than the others. Some of the other players would smile and say to me, "Gabriela, that wall used to be straight before you came to the Club. Now, because of such hard playing, you have 'bent' the wall!" This was very funny, and we all laughed.

At home we had our own patio walls. There were no lines of people, and no waiting. Here I could play any time I wanted. There were actually three walls in our patio, one on each side and one in the front. My favorite wall was the one in the front. My game could only be played on the best walls. I would fantasize for hours about the walls in our neighborhood. My mind sought out walls that didn't have any cracks in them. The smoother the wall, the better. Walls with bumps and cracks in them made the ball bounce back funny, like the "bent" wall at the Club. Brick walls were the worst! Smooth walls made the balls come back faster and straighter. Everywhere all I could see were walls! I would think, "I could really use that wall!" Or, "That wall looks perfect! No bumps! No lines!"

Most evenings at home after dinner I couldn't wait to go play again. As soon as I finished dinner, I would race outside to our patio wall.

My parents usually tried to put up with the constant banging of the ball against the wall, but I guess that sometimes it got to be too much for them. My mother might call out, "Please, Gaby! You're giving me a headache!"

Osvaldo would shout, "I can't concentrate on my homework with all that banging!" even though I knew he was really watching television.

I decided that if I were smart I should start playing as much as I could on our patio walls. I made my own game of hitting the tennis ball back and forth against walls. I moved from one wall to another, then another, and then back to the first. I went up and down the walls, until I had played and conquered every square inch of their surfaces. These walls were perfect for me. They didn't stand a chance!

I was probably the best six-year-old wall expert in all of Argentina! Maybe in all of South America!

I would play for hours on these walls. They were some of the best playmates I ever had. They never complained about the banging, they never got tired, and they were ready to play any time I was. I had no sense of time. I was surprised when it started to get dark and I could hardly see the ball anymore. If it didn't get dark, I probably would have played twenty-four hours a day. I lived to hit that ball against the wall in the evening, and over the net at the club by day. This was one of the most exciting times of my life! It was something marvelous to have this great toy! I was forever outside defeating opponents at the club when I could get there, and when I couldn't, I'd challenge and defeat every wall in sight!

4

My New World of Tennis

From the time I was six until I was eight years old, I played every spare minute. When I couldn't play, I read about famous players or watched them play on TV. I was fascinated by anything about tennis. One Saturday afternoon, some friends and I were at my house watching tennis on TV. We saw Guillermo Vilas, the most famous tennis star in Argentina. I was amazed with the way he hit the ball. We watched him run and leap for it, and he always got it into the opponent's court at exactly the right place. He was lightning on the court.

The audience got so excited that they started chanting, "Guee-yare-mo! Guee-yare-mo! Guee-yare-mo!" It was the first time I had ever heard a tennis crowd chant a great player's name. It wouldn't be the last.

Guillermo Vilas became my first guide, a model for me to pattern myself after as I matured. I loved watching him play. When I played, I imagined that I would some day hit the ball just as he hit it. I could see myself flying toward the net, stretching, and making the kind of perfect return down the line Guillermo could make!

Several friends of my parents had watched me play at the River Plate Club. They said, "Osvaldo (that was my father's name too), Gaby is no ordinary child tennis player. She has excellent coordination, quickness and strength for someone her age. And she seems to have a real feel for the game! She's far better than anyone we've ever seen before. Have you considered getting her professional tennis training?"

My father answered, "You know, I've thought about it. I'll talk to my wife tonight, and if she agrees and if Gaby wants to, I'll make the arrangements."

My mother agreed. When my father asked me if I wanted to, I laughed with joy. I think he knew my answer before he asked me.

The next day my father took me to meet Mr. Daniel Fidalgo. This was my first meeting with a professional teacher. My father had to hold my hand all the time he was talking with Mr. Fidalgo, because I was so very excited about meeting him.

5

The Tennis School

Mr. Fidalgo had a tennis school at the River Plate Club set up just for children. There were nearly a hundred girls and boys in his school, from six years old up to fifteen. I was one of the youngest. He knew just about everything there was to know about tennis and he worked really well with children. I was only six and a half at the time, but I can remember he was very kind to the other kids and me. He never made us do things for which we weren't ready.

To help us learn good tennis, Mr. Fidalgo taught us all the basic tennis moves. He had us playing each other over and over again, until we became excellent in our play. He had also developed a bunch of "special" games to help us learn some of the more difficult moves. These were more complicated than my wall games. His games helped teach us many more tennis techniques and rules.

"I teach you games," he said one day, "so you can learn tennis. But you must always remember that tennis is a game too, and should be played because it's fun. The more you enjoy the game, the better you will be. And the better you become, the more you will enjoy the game. So, children, play for the joy of it!"

Even his name was fun. He told us his nick-name was "Palito," (pah-lee-toe) which is Spanish for "little stick." This name was right for him because he was so skinny, skinny as a stick. It was a fun name "Palito," and we all learned to love it.

In one of his most popular games, Mr. Fidalgo would have ten or twelve children with their tennis racquets line up at the baseline — that's the back line of the tennis court — on one side of the net. He would be on the other side. He would hit the ball over the net to each of us, one at a time. We had to hit the ball back to him.

If we succeeded, he would call out, "Good shot! Fine volley!"

If we didn't make a good return, we had to get out of line. He didn't say anything then.

This continued until only one person was left, and that was the winner. I remember many times when we played this game that I was the last person left in the line.

"Wow!" I thought, "this is pretty easy — and a lot more fun than beating my poor patio wall!"

I really learned to love and respect Mr. Fidalgo. He was great teacher, a teacher who really knew how to work with children. Mr.

Fidalgo knew the importance of having fun. He was a great trainer who never pushed the young children beyond their abilities. He let us all develop at our own rate of learning. And whatever he did, he made sure that we would have fun. We improved every day because we got to practice without pressure, and in a fun way. And in having fun, we all became better tennis players. Even the slowest and worst of us improved. It was a great time for all of us.

Mr. Fidalgo was right. The better I got with his training, the more I enjoyed tennis, and the more I enjoyed tennis, the harder I worked to improve my game.

Although I was only seven and a half years old, I had discovered what I loved most in life — playing tennis. I never thought about a career as a tennis player then. I was too young for that. All I knew was that I loved tennis and I wanted it always to be a part of my life, maybe even the center of my life. I am so thankful to you, Mr. Fidalgo, for caring so much for me and for all the other kids in your School for Tennis. You taught me more than you'll ever know.

6

Analia Spills the Beans

After about a year and a half at the Tennis School, I started playing in the local tournaments in Argentina. I was in the third grade at my regular school. My mother, Beatriz, would pick me up from school around eleven or noon to drive me to the tournaments. I didn't want to tell any of my school friends about my tennis playing. I didn't want them to think I was anything special because I really didn't see myself that way. But I was afraid that if the kids knew I was playing in tournaments, they might think that *I* thought that I was somehow "special" or better than they were. And also, I was kind of shy. Tennis was my joy, and I only played for my own satisfaction. I wanted to avoid jealousies and misunderstandings, so I kept my tennis playing and the tournaments a secret from my schoolmates for a long time.

I was involved in tournaments for about a year before my secret was discovered. I was eight

years old. It happened one day after I had won
a local tournament. My tennis match victory was
written up in all the local papers. One of my
friends, Analia, came to school one morning
all excited, waving a copy of a local newspaper.

She ran up to me and said, "Hey! You're some
kind of tennis star, aren't you? Isn't this you in
the newspaper? We read about you winning a
giant tennis tournament against girls a lot older
than you. *Is this really you?*"

Then she yelled for all the other kids to hear,
"Hey, I've been sitting next to a famous tennis
star all this time! How come you never told us
you were a tennis star?"

I just blushed. Boy! Did I blush!

From that moment on, my secret was out.
Analia had "spilled the beans" all over the place.
Now everybody at school knew! Everyone was
really friendly, not at all jealous, and was curious
about my formerly secret life of tennis. This was
much different from what I had imagined. I
started to relax and could now be proud about
my successes with my friends. I think they
became my very first and my most loyal fans. It
was a good feeling for them — and a great relief
for me!

7

My First Lesson for Life

When I was nine years old, I became the **Number One Player** in the *"Infantiles"* or child tennis league in Argentina. Then, I moved up to the *"Menores"* or minor leagues, which is for young people under fourteen. When I was twelve, I graduated again, this time to the *"Cadetes"* or cadet level for girls sixteen years old and younger. This was a great honor for me, since I was always the youngest girl in all of these tournament categories.

I loved playing and going to the tournaments. I continued to go and always played my best. I especially loved the challenge of playing girls older and bigger than I was. It made me play harder, and the harder I played, the better I got.

But tournaments weren't enough. I continued to practice and to learn. I would say to myself, "Yes, I'm a good tennis player, but there are two things better than good. One of them is *better*. The other one is *best*."

My First Lesson for Life

Even though I was playing in this, and in other major tournaments, I never thought I was anyone special. Yes, winning was good, but it was playing well that was the greatest joy! I was always happy and very confident. But I never believed I was any sort of marvelous thing. I was just a young tennis player in love with the game.

It was at this time that I learned a very important lesson in life. I had always loved tennis. Now, at ten years old, I had been playing almost half my life. It was my personal pleasure to play. I never thought that just winning was important as a goal. *What was important was knowing that I had done my absolute best.* So my first goal was always to play my best. It was through this feeling about the game — and in life — *always to try my best,* that winning happened at all. If I had stopped to think about how great I was doing, or to worry about it, I might not have been able to concentrate. Without good concentration it would be very difficult to face and to overcome the next, even harder challenge, and the next, and the one after that.

8

The Training Camp

During one of my South American tournaments, I met Patricio Apey. Mr. Apey was a renowned tennis coach from Chile who had moved to Florida in the United States. He was now living near Miami where he had a famous training camp for young tennis players. The camp itself was on a little island or key off the coast of Florida.

Mr. Apey said, "Your playing is very good, Gabriela, but you can really profit by more professional training. You have the look of a great tennis player."

I couldn't help smiling at the compliment. It felt so good. I was finally able to murmur a bashful, "Thank you."

Several months later as I came in from school, my mother called, "Gaby! Gaby! There's a letter for you from the United States! Quick! Open it!"

I ripped the letter open and read it. It was from Patricio Apey.

"Mother, he's invited me to train with him at his tennis camp! Fantastic!"

The Training Camp

That night my family and I discussed this opportunity. We'd always been a close and loving family and always made important decisions together. It was agreed that this was a chance not to be missed. Until that time, I had only local training and practice in Buenos Aires with Mr. Fidalgo. And now Patricio Apey's invitation to train with him in Florida! This could open the door for many great opportunities in the future.

I was only twelve when I went to train in Florida. Luckily I didn't have to travel by myself. Another young tennis player, Mercedes Paz, who was my friend, also went to Mr. Apey's tennis camp. It was a great comfort to my family and to me to have an Argentinean girl with me.

This was my first time to train and practice outside of South America with players from many different countries around the world. I was very nervous. I wondered if I'd measure up. I wondered if they'd like me. I worried that I wouldn't like them. What I discovered was that they too loved the game, that they too wanted to improve, and that they too worried about the same things I did. We got along great! In later years many of them went on to become famous tennis players themselves. I met them often on my tours and we had fun reunions.

I first went to the training camp for three months between tournaments. I would come back after a tournament to train and practice some more. For example, I played in the U.S. Open, the most important tournament in the United States, and then returned to the training camp to continue working on my game. Then I would leave again for another tournament, and back again to train some more.

9

———◦|◦———

My First U.S. Open

At the 1984 U.S. Open tournament in New York, I had the opportunity to play against a great tennis star, Helena Sukova. Helena was a "seed" player, which meant that she was one of the top ten players in the world of women's tennis. I had won two side court matches. These wins made me eligible to play against Helena.

After my victories on the side courts, I was scheduled to play Helena in the Stadium on main court. This was the biggest court on which I ever played, and I was very excited to be there. Also, I was a little nervous. I couldn't believe it. The Stadium court seated so many more people than the outside courts!

There were ten thousand people in the seats, all quiet and looking straight at me. But no matter what was happening around me, I kept my concentration on my tennis. In fact, if you were to ask me if there were a lot of people in the stands, I can say yes, but I was not even sure if they were standing or sitting, if the seats were completely full, or if they were empty. I concentrated so deeply that the only thing that mattered was my tennis. It was my joy, and my only desire was to play well and have a good time. The game was during the daytime and the temperature was hot, about 82° F. Sometimes, when it is very hot and humid, you start sweating even before the playing starts.

This game was exciting to me in other ways. It was the very first time I had so much attention except in Argentina in the *"Menores"* league. Television cameras were sending pictures of us around the world, so everyone could watch Helena and me play. We gave them a good show, because it was a very long, hard match. After this, I began playing more professional matches and won quite a few of them.

There were tennis lessons every day and body conditioning and practice, practice, and then, just for a change, more practice. Mr. Apey had a very large house where we all stayed. Yes, we were kids from all over the world who had come to train with Mr. Apey, but we were just ten to four- teen years old, and we made sure that there was more to life than just training and tennis!

All the girls stayed in one big dormitory room. There were usually eight to ten of us. It was quite crazy! We were always playing little jokes on each other. Mr. Apey and the other coaches didn't know anything about all the funny things we girls did. It was lots of fun and a very happy time for all of us, and we managed to stay friends no matter how bad the jokes were.

10

The Disappearing Mattresses

One time, during the first week at camp, there was the mystery of the disappearing mattresses. Our beds were made up of two parts, the soft mattress on top, and the hard springs underneath. One day I came in especially sore and tired and was longing to lie down. I saw it! There it was! My wonderful, soft bed! I made a flying leap toward it! Oh, did I need to stretch out and relax for a while! And then — thump!! I hit hard springs! My feather-soft mattress! It was gone! I was stunned, amazed, disappointed — and I knew that I had been had by some jokester! My poor stomach would be sore for a week. I found my mattress out in the back of the dormitory.

No! Any girls who had played this joke on me weren't going to get away with it. No sir! Because I was the first one back from practice, I was alone in the room. I decided that maybe the other girls would like to check out the hard springs too. It took me just five minutes to hide nine mattresses next to mine in back of the dormitory! That was probably a new world record for mattress hiding! I put clean bed sheets over the hard springs to cover them.

Exactly one minute later the other girls came in from practice. It took just thirty seconds for them to figure out the problem. After a few loud thumps, head banging, groans, and lots of confusion, we all saw the joke, and ten girls laughed so hard that Mr. Apey came in to see what was going on! We were always doing things like that.

11

Cleaning Up
at the Camp

One day, in about our third week, I was laundering my clothes in the washing machine. To help Mercedes, who had come to the camp with me from Argentina, I put her clothes in with mine. I waited until the clothes were washed and then I took them out. Something was funny. The clothes all looked weird. Her clothes were originally in solid colors, blues and reds. After the wash, however, they came out with swirls of blue mixed with red and purple. They looked bruised all over, as if they had been in an accident! I didn't know what happened.

When I showed the clothes to Mercedes, her face turned almost the same colors as her clothes. For some reason she was really upset that all her clothes had changed colors. She was yelling and howling about it, and saying stuff like "How could you put my clothes in there?" and "Who taught you how to wash clothes?"

"Wow!" I thought. "She sure doesn't appreciate favors! The next time she can do her own laundry."

12

The Chocolate Surprise

Of all the tricks and games we played on each other at the camp, there is one that I will absolutely never forget. Sometimes I seem pretty serious, and I guess it's more fun to play pranks on serious people than on people who are less serious.

This trick had to do with my passion for sweet chocolate candies. I had just turned thirteen. It was my habit to grab a few chocolates between training and meals, so I bought this big paper bag filled with chocolates and placed it next to my bed. Next to tennis, I loved chocolate the most.

Just after training one day I went directly to my chocolate bag to have a little candy. I think my body craved the sugar to replace the energy I used in playing the game. Anyway, on this day I walked over to my bag of chocolates, reached in and grabbed one. It tasted great. Rich, creamy, sweet milk chocolate that just melted in my mouth! Yum, Yum, Yummy! I slowly finished it and reached in for another. This one felt strange. It was soft on one side, hard on the other, and had little strings or wires sticking out of it! I pulled it out of the bag fast! It was a whopping big brown cockroach! It started to wiggle, and then it jumped out of my hand and scurried under the bed, disappearing to who knows where. What a surprise! I knew someone had put that cockroach into the bag.

"Oh, thanks a lot! What a delicious gift!" I said to my friends, who were by now all cracking up about it. I was so angry at them! "That's no joke!" I told them.

They were a little embarrassed and apologized, but said, yes it was most certainly a joke. I thought about it for a while, pictured what I must have looked like pulling the big cockroach out of the bag, and had to laugh too.

"Well," I said slowly, "maybe it was a joke — a real tiny one."

From that time on, however, I always bought smaller bags of chocolates so I could finish them before another "chocolate cockroach" could share in the sweets.

13

My Second Lesson for Life

Going to the training camp was the first time that I had left home for more than a few days. It was a very big step for me. Many of my friends in Argentina said that they would be very scared to leave home at twelve years old. But I wasn't. I had already played in tournaments all over Argentina and South America for several years. My brother and parents had usually been with me, but not always. I was comfortable traveling alone. I was confident and trusting enough in other people so that, when I left for Miami, there was no fear at all. And my friend Mercedes was with me. There was no time to think about being scared. I was also eager to see and learn about another country, the United States.

All of this was very exciting, and I couldn't wait to leave. For me, it became a great new adventure. I was really looking forward to it. After all, this was tennis. And for me, tennis was everything. With this as my goal and my life, I felt happy and secure. This was the second real understanding in my life: *Courage comes from inside yourself. When you know your goal, and pursue that above everything else, you will have the courage to do anything or be anything you wish.* That knowledge has stayed with me ever since.

14

The First Overseas Tour

Things went very well in the Florida training camp — except, of course, for that cockroach incident. We learned much about the techniques and strategies of tennis, and I was progressing well in all my tournaments. I was traveling more as well, and I planned to make tennis a permanent part of my life. I talked seriously with my parents many times about continuing my traveling so that I could play tournaments all around the world. It is usual that the players would attend a tournament in one country, then travel to another and another. Groups of tournament players like myself would travel together to each country to play.

My parents agreed that it was worth trying a foreign tour and gave me permission to go if I could find a dependable traveling companion.

My father said, "Let's just see how it goes. If you do well, then you can continue. If things don't go well, you'll come back to Argentina and return to school. Agreed?"

But now there was that really big question: Who would travel with me? I was only thirteen and still too young to travel by myself for more than a short time. The European trip would last over one month.

My parents were working all the time, so they couldn't travel with me. We decided that I would travel with my friend Mercedes Paz from the training camp. Mercedes was just sixteen. Like me, this was her first big trip away from home. She and I were very excited about traveling, and we raced to get our things together.

We made all the travel arrangements and packed for the trip. On the day of the flight, our parents drove us to the airport and stayed with us for what seemed like hours before we could board the plane. I think they were really worried about us but they tried not to show it. They didn't succeed very well. Finally Mercedes and I got our seat assignments together, picked up our racquets — we always hand carried them — and hugged and kissed our parents goodbye. We then set off down a long, dark passage with a sign over it reading *CUSTOMS*.

15

The Customs Officer

As soon as we arrived at the customs window, we met a uniformed man, the Customs Agent. He looked at us very seriously.

He asked, "Where are you young ladies going all by yourselves?" He made it sound as if we were doing something wrong.

Mercedes answered, "We're tennis players. We're going to South Africa for a week of tournaments, and then to Europe."

He picked up our passports, looked at them, looked at me, and looked at Mercedes. Then, he stamped our passports with a big diamond-shaped ink mark, handed them back to us, and pointed the way to the terminal section where we would board the plane. I was happy to be finally leaving for a new adventure. It was both strange and exciting, and I couldn't wait to see what happened next.

16

My First Long Flight

We were then rushed into the plane. After storing our racquets in the overhead compartment, we took our seats. It was all so hurried, and we now tried to calm down from all the excitement. My seat was next to a window on the right side. From my window, I could see the baggage being loaded, bag by bag, into the side of the plane. I saw Mercedes' suitcase, then mine, and some of our gear. It was a big plane, like a giant boat, with hundreds of people filling all the seats. A nice stewardess came over and adjusted our seat belts. She then explained the flight to us. She said we would be first going to Cape Town, South Africa. It was going to be a long trip, more than twelve hours.

After a few minutes, the plane took off. It was like a roller coaster, except we didn't go down, just up. As we looked out the window, we could see the airport and all the other planes. The higher we went, the smaller they became, and soon we were too far away to see anything. It was a dark and cloudy day, but after a while the plane darted through the clouds and let the sun shine in the small windows in our cabin. It was really strange to suddenly see the sky above, and the clouds and earth getting smaller below us.

17

Cape Town

We were very tired. After landing, we went through South African customs, gathered all our stuff, and took the airport bus into the city. We found a small hotel where we stayed for two days. I called my family from the hotel phone. Everybody was happy to hear from me. Mercedes also called her family. The next day we did a little tour of the city, and then rested. The following day, our second day in South Africa, we started our week of tournaments. Following that, we continued on our travels to Europe, where the real "fun" started.

This time, we would be flying directly into Charles DeGaulle Airport near Paris. We had been flying for nearly a full day, and now it was morning. In France, we began our experiences on the trains of Europe.

18

Trains, Trains Everywhere

We started out from the central train station. Our tour schedules had us in different cities on different days. To be at the tournament cities on time, we had to arrange a very complicated travel schedule. The trains themselves were very similar to those in Argentina. The cars were organized as "smoking" or "nonsmoking," and "first class" or "second class." Each car had several compartments where people could sit. Usually there were three seats on each side of the compartment. This allowed up to six adults to sit comfortably. Like the planes, there were little overhead racks where we could put our luggage during the trip. If the racks were full, we had to put our stuff on the floor or on our seats.

Getting our bags on the trains was always a lot of work. We first had to lift every piece through the narrow doors. Then, we had to drag them down the narrow aisles to the compartments. In the compartments, we had to lift the

bags up about six feet high to fit on the racks.
So it was lots of work to move on and off these
trains. Sometimes, because of the location of the
city, we would have to take two or three different
trains in the same day to get to our next destination. Other times, it was just a short distance
away. And each time we changed trains we had
to carry our heavy luggage full of tennis gear
and clothes with us.

There was a lot of pressure for us to be on
time in the tournament cities. If we were late,
we could miss the event entirely. We had to rush.
Often there was hardly enough time to finish
a match, take the train to the next location, find
a hotel, get enough sleep before the next match,
get ready, and then catch the next train after that
match to the next event. This is why we planned
our train traveling very carefully. We felt sort of
like a traveling circus, because we were only in
one place long enough to sleep, play the match,
and then take another train for the next tournament.

This time there was no family to protect me,
and no helpful advice from friends to comfort me
in these strange new places. I became very aware
at times that I was only a thirteen year old kid.

We traveled this way for more than a month.
Many times we were homesick, and sometimes
even a little scared. This wasn't like going to the
Florida training camp. There I was never scared.

I had my friends and Mr. Apey watching out for us. But here in Europe it was very different. No one knew us, and, except for Mercedes, I couldn't speak to anyone. No one seemed to know Spanish. However, I was able to use the English I learned in the United States to find my way around. But this was still difficult. It was like being on Mars.

We missed our family and friends so much that we cried every day and every night. I missed my mom and dad more than anything. Mercedes missed hers as well. This period was one of the most difficult times of my life because for the first time I had no one to count on but myself and Mercedes. Sure, we were great friends, but it's not like being at home with your family.

I can't tell you how many times either Mercedes or I would say, "When will this tour be over? I can't wait to get home to my folks, my house, my own bed! How I hate hotels! And trains! Ugh!"

Still, we managed to support each other. When one of us was low or really homesick, the other one was up and able to help the other person. If she would start to cry, I would tell her that it would be over soon and we could be with our friends and family in a little while. And so it was that we helped each other survive in these foreign places where we couldn't even speak the language and had no one to talk to but ourselves.

We kept talking to each other about how we needed to survive and be well and be brave in order to live our dreams of playing professional tennis.

19

Misfortune Strikes

We had a miserable experience two weeks after leaving home. We had just finished a tournament in the French city of Nice and were now traveling to Genoa, Italy, then on to another city for the next tournament. We were on several trains that day, first in one station, then in another, changing four or five times. We traveled all day and into the night. When we finally arrived at our destination, it was stormy and cold. We rushed to get our bags and tennis gear off the train before it pulled out for the next station. We both got soaked lugging our baggage in the cold, pouring rain. Fortunately, we found a mini-taxi nearby that would bring us to our hotel. We would have been stuck at the station if that taxi hadn't been there.

The hotel was close by the Genoa station. It was old and looked as if it had been battered in the two world wars and a revolution or two. The building was made of decaying stone that was covered with mustard-brown mold. The antique walls glistened, wet with the raindrops splashing off in all directions. It was three stories high, and had ugly little gargoyle water spouts on the roof gushing water all over the street — and onto us — below. We were afraid to go inside.

Our taxi driver, who spoke English and some Spanish mixed in with Italian when those other languages failed him, assured us it was okay.

He said, "The hotel is very old, over a hundred years, but the rooms are clean and the price is good. You will find no better at this time of night." He was very kind and seemed really concerned about us.

It was nearly ten p.m., and we were very tired. We went into the hotel. The taxi driver helped us carry our stuff inside. We went to the front desk which was more like a kitchen table, and met the manager, a very old woman.

"May we have a double room please?" I asked in Spanish.

She looked at us blankly. I think she said, "What?" in Italian.

"She is very old — eighty-seven at least," the taxi driver said, "and doesn't speak either English or Spanish, but it doesn't matter since she's quite deaf and couldn't hear you no matter what language you spoke. But she can still work. She is still a hard worker."

I looked at the old woman with great admiration. I wanted to be like that when I was eighty-seven, except I didn't want to be deaf. We wondered which room she had been born in because she and the hotel were so similar — decrepit on the outside, but clean and sturdy on the inside.

The taxi driver smiled with pride at the old manager and helped us with all the check-in procedures. We both managed tired smiles toward him and the old woman, said good night, and trudged upstairs three flights with our bags. We opened the creaky door, dropped our bags, fell onto the beds, and dropped instantly to sleep.

The next morning I woke up as usual. There was no tennis game that day, so there was no big rush. Suddenly, as I turned my head on my pillow, a sharp, stabbing pain knifed through my left ear. I screamed! I couldn't get up. Every move made the pain worse, so I just lay there quietly. I was dizzy, I could barely talk, the pain was horrible. I had the worst earache of my life. I really needed my parents. Here was something beyond my control that they would be able to fix. The pain was so bad that I thought I was going to die in this old hotel in this strange foreign country. Being this far away from home now seemed like the worst nightmare I have ever experienced. My father and mother would have been so helpful at a time like this. I remembered how nice it would be to be at home. I never appreciated them more than at this point.

Mercedes, great friend that she was, tried to

talk with the manager. This was useless, so Mercedes ran out of the hotel and into the streets in a panic. She was desperate to find help for me. She tried to speak Italian which is very close to Spanish and a little like Portuguese, and was finally able to get me some medicine from a local pharmacy. I never appreciated anyone as much as I appreciated Mercedes that day. She was the best friend a person could have.

By the next morning, after lots of care by Mercedes and plenty of rest and hot food, my ear infection was totally gone. But was that ever scary! And was I ever relieved when that pain went away—never had I been so scared that far from home.

20

The Missing Purse

The tournament in Genoa went well. From there, we got back on the train and headed to Milan. It was on that trip that something terrible happened. Mercedes always traveled with a waist purse attached to her belt. This was a special purse where she kept her credit cards, her money and her passport. It was always around her waist, a kind of tummy safe for her valuables. On the way to Milan, her belt broke and the purse dropped off. Mercedes caught the falling purse before it hit the floor. She put both the broken belt and her purse into another bag in order to get it repaired in Milan. When we got to the station where we had to change trains, we rushed to get all our luggage and tennis gear off the train before the new passengers could get on. The train only stopped for about a minute and we had to move as fast as we could before it started again. In order to get to Milan on time that day, we had to make four — *four!* — changes of trains.

On our third train toward Milan, we were getting hungry. We decided to buy some crackers

and milk from one of those food sellers who go
up and down the aisles on Italian trains.
Mercedes went to pay the man.

Suddenly, alarmed, she jumped out of her
seat, and half screaming and half moaning, said,
"My purse! My money purse! I can't find it!"

All her travelers checks, credit cards, cash
and documents were missing. There was no way
we could go back and search two or three
different trains. We weren't even sure how many
train rides ago it was that she lost her purse. We
spent the next two days making phone calls home
trying to get money for Mercedes. All during that
time I tried to help her as much as I could.

"Don't worry," I told her. "We're friends.
You're welcome to anything I have — money,
credit cards, whatever. We'll get through this
together just as we did when I had that earache."

We were lucky that we did not have another
tournament for the next few days. That allowed
Mercedes time to arrange for the replacement
of all her lost things. We were certainly relieved
when money from home finally arrived for her
in Milan, and her passport was replaced.

Much of our traveling was fun, but there were
real difficulties and hardships. My earache and
Mercedes' lost purse were just a couple of examples. It was a very exciting, very scary and
always a challenging trip. But in the entire month
of traveling, we always managed to solve our

Playing at one of my first tournaments in Buenos Aires, Argentina. Age 8.

Playing at the same tournament as the photo on the left. Age 8.

My mother is presenting me with a trophy at a special ceremony at The River Plate Club in Buenos Aires. Age 8.

Above: Playing hard for the River Plate Club against another local tennis club in Argentina. Age 9.

Right: Posing at a tournament competition in Buenos Aires. Age 9.

*Arriving
at another
tournament
in Venezuela.
Age 11.*

*Right: Shown volleying
at the National Tennis
Tournament in
Argentina. Age 10.*

Playing at another tournament in Argentina. Age 11.

Shown pointing to my achievement of becoming Number One in my category. This was in the famous "Banana Bowl" tournament in Sao Paulo, Brazil. I was 11 years old.

52

Playing at a tournament in Monte Carlo, Monaco during my first Overseas trip to Europe with Mercedes Paz. I had just turned 14 years old.

At home in Buenos Aires with trophies won during my first Overseas trip with Mercedes. Age 14 ¹/₂.

Resting after winning a local game at The River Plate Club. Age 15.

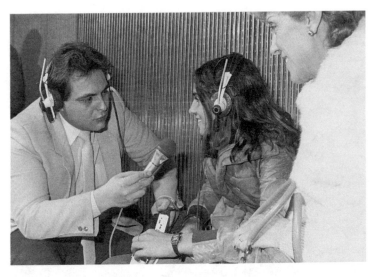

Press interview in Ezeiza International Airport in Buenos Aires upon arrival from European tour, 1984

Having fun at Patricio Apey's Miami home. From left to right: Patricio's father (top), me, my brother Osvaldo, and Mercedes (bottom left).

Arriving in Buenos Aires with my father (top right) from European tour. Shown being welcomed by my mother (bottom left), and my brother Osvaldo (top left)

In Miami with Dick Dell, my agent (left) and Carlos Kirmayr, my coach, 1992.

problems. It seemed like the more problems we solved, the easier travel became. It was a great learning experience, which I knew would prepare me for the next part of my life.

21

My Third Lesson for Life

Most important of all, however, was the fact that I found out I could actually handle the travel. I knew I was a good enough tennis player, but it takes a lot more than that to be a successful professional. You had to be able to put up with discomfort, tricky schedules, strange food, bad food, awful food, lumpy hotel beds, achy muscles, loneliness and homesickness. I had done it. I had come through. I could be tough facing hardships when I had to be, and I could be tender with people. That was important to me.

I learned a lot during this time. I had faced all the fears, and didn't let anything stop me. Hardships forced me to learn how to face new challenges, and that helped me to grow up. *I learned that once you have faced a difficult experience in your life, you can handle other difficult experiences much more easily.* So even though traveling by myself was the scariest thing I had ever done, I would now be able to handle

59

anything else that would come up in my life.

My life changed forever after that month in Europe. *I had learned about my inner strengths, and realized that I could now do anything I wanted. I lost my fear of things, and realized that I could draw on my new strength whenever I needed it.* I shall never forget it. From that time onward, everything became easy for me. I didn't know it at the time, but I had forged a new life for myself. That new life would be the greatest thing that would ever happen to me. That new life was a life of tennis.

22

Coming Home

When Mercedes and I were traveling around Europe, we were both getting lots of experiences in the big international tournaments. The first big match was at the French Open, near Paris. We had been traveling almost a month, and we were very homesick.

My father, whom I missed very much, joined us on the tour in the city of Alessandria, Italy. He had gotten a vacation from his job. I remember him arriving at our little hotel. I was eagerly waiting for him in the hotel lobby. Finally his taxi drove up, and there he was!

I ran to him and he enfolded me in his arms in a great big hug and a kiss on the cheek. My father is a big, very handsome man. He's a six foot two inches tall teddy bear of a man who seems always to be in a good mood. After being away from home for so long, and as homesick as I was, seeing my father was like sunshine after a long storm. It felt so good to be "home" again. Of course, I missed my mother and big brother and friends, but having my father there with me took away much of my loneliness.

My father and I talked about the busy
schedule in Italy. I had been playing all the
smaller tournaments around Italy and France and
had three more in Italy before the French Open.
After that there would be Wimbledon in England,
and then a bunch more in several other European
countries.

Although I was having a successful tour —
I had won many of the tournaments I entered —
I was getting tired and the schedule ahead of me
seemed to be so much! My father and I talked it
over and decided I had been away long enough.
After the French Open I would return to my
beloved Argentina. Mercedes would continue on
the tour without me. My father traveled with me
for the three remaining tournaments. I continued
to do well, again mostly winning. And then it was
time for me to go home.

23

Bienvenida, Gabriela!

Going home after such a long time away was strange. I felt that I had been on a strange planet and was at long last returning to Mother Earth. The constant push and shove we had on the tour were now gone. My father arranged all the travel plans, and soon after the French Open, we were heading back. I was so tired, it seemed as if I were drifting around in a dream, the dream of going home. I could relax on the plane. I could read a book, or watch a movie and I didn't have to worry about catching the next train or finding a place to sleep that night.

The long plane trip home was very smooth. I remembered back to when Mercedes and I left Argentina for the European tour. Then it was all strange and exciting and a little scary. That flight had been bumpy. Now this flight home with my father was smooth and relaxing. I ended up sleeping in my chair for most of the trip.

After many hours, the plane finally arrived in Buenos Aires. We got off the plane and picked up our stuff from the baggage counter. Then we went through Argentine customs. I showed my passport to the customs inspector. He looked up at me, jumped back, and saluted — all without saying a word! I thought, "This is very strange! Customs inspectors are some of the most serious men in the world! This one is sure weird!"

My father saw my puzzlement. "I'm sure he's only joking," he said.

We came out of Customs with our bags using one of these little metal carts like the ones in supermarkets. Everything, my father's bag and all my stuff, was piled on top of it. It was a lot of stuff, but we managed it okay. We pushed the cart up a little ramp and turned a corner to the "greeting" area where people meet and greet incoming passengers. I looked around and saw thousands of people jammed into this big room. I had not seen this at the other airports or at the train stations in Europe or even at the tournaments, which were always bustling with people.

"Hey," I said to my father, "Something's going on here. Let's get out of the way before whoever they're waiting for arrives. It must be a politician or a rock star or the Pope!"

My father smiled and said, "Gabriela, take a closer look at the people! They're all looking at you!"

Suddenly, I stopped pushing the cart and looked around at the people in the crowd. My face turned red! There were my friends, my mother, my brother and uncle, and so many schoolmates! And so many other people I didn't know! People holding signs which read **"Welcome Home Gaby"** or **"Argentina's Greatest Young Tennis Star!"** It was a giant party and I was at the center of it! Some were yelling my nickname, "Gaby! Gaby! Gaby!" I remembered how as a little girl those years before I saw people on television chanting for Guillermo Vilas, and suddenly I felt so proud and such a rush of love for the Argentinean people!

When the crowds saw us, they rushed forward like a great flood of people. There were newspaper reporters and TV cameras too. I never knew they were going to be there. Nobody told me. It was a giant surprise! It felt like all of Argentina had come to the airport to welcome me home!

For two hours we had TV and newspaper interviews at the airport. My eyes hurt from the many flash cameras taking our pictures. At last we got to the car and drove out of the airport. What an experience! For the first time in my life I was doing interviews with reporters, and I was only thirteen! But I was tired. I was so happy to get away from the crowd and the reporters. I was really looking forward to climbing into my own bed at home for a very long sleep.

But my sleep had to wait. More reporters were waiting at the house. It was crazy. All of

them wanted my story of what happened in
Europe, and how it felt to be a tennis star.

"Actually," I said wearily, "I feel the same. I'm
the same Gabriela who loves to play tennis, who
loves her family, and who would love to get some
sleep."

A reporter said, "The people want to read
about you, Gabriela. You are their hero, and now
you're not only famous in your own country, but
around the world! All of Argentina is proud of you
and wants to know all about you! Please tell us
about your tours. We need to know."

The reporters were all so nice, but also very
eager. Each would ask me questions about how
I played, or how the other person played. They
wanted to know what was my best shot, or my
worst, how I felt when I won, or when I didn't win.

One asked, "Were you aware that you had
become famous in Argentina?"

I answered, "No, not until I arrived at the
airport today! What a surprise! I'm so thrilled!"

I didn't tell them about all the hardships of the
travel or about the crying and loneliness or about
my miserable earache. I didn't feel they would
have wanted to hear all those depressing things.
The reporters continued to come to my house all
the rest of that first day. And the next day they
came early in the morning, and continued until
late in the evening. For days the house was
always full of people wanting interviews. I

couldn't say "no" to the reporters. This was all so new an experience.

I had just got my first idea of what it was like to be considered important. I was so young. I never realized when we were racing to trains and fighting fear and discomfort in Europe that it would lead to this. I wasn't playing for fame, but for fun.

All our hard work and determination to finish the tournaments, win or lose, certainly was far from my mind that day. This was a lot of excitement. I tried to help satisfy the reporters by answering questions and letting them take pictures because, even though it was often very tiring, I knew that they too had a job to do. I was starting to like all the attention. It was a great new fun part of my world of tennis. It could be a lot of fun, but I was happy when they finally left.

After thinking about this, I finally understood that the excitement and attention were all part of playing tennis. And for me, everything and anything associated with tennis had to be good. When I looked at it like that, it became a very happy thing, to be interviewed about my tennis and how I played. I also loved seeing myself in the magazines and newspapers. I knew then that tennis had been good to me, and I wanted nothing more than to be good for tennis.

24

Professional Tennis

I began to play as a professional in the majors when I was fifteen. Some of the major tournaments in which I played were in the U.S. Open in New York, the Virginia Slims Tournament, and several others in Los Angeles, Miami, and Canada. Some of these tournaments took me back to Europe. I worked with Patricio Apey on these tours. He was a wonderful teacher and was extremely helpful in directing my career. One day he called me aside and said, "Gaby, you're becoming quite a successful athlete. I think it's time you had a professional agent to help you."

"Help me how? What can an agent do?"

Mr. Apey replied, "He schedules tours for you, arranges hotels, takes care of all sorts of things. And, very importantly, he takes care of your financial interests for you."

"I don't know anyone who can do that. Do you?"

"I think I do. Dick Dell with the ProServ Group. He's a nice guy, honest, and really knows the business. He was a professional tennis player himself for years, and also a successful lawyer. Let me introduce him to you."

It was good meeting and working with Dick, and finally to have a professional guide to help direct my career.

Doing the professional tours was lots of fun and much more challenging to me. The other players were older and more experienced. This made me work harder to compete against them. By playing these more experienced professionals, I was able to improve my game greatly. I became physically and mentally stronger. I learned to fight harder. I was very pleased with my continuing improvement. Playing professional tennis was what I wanted to do for the rest of my life.

During one particular tournament in Argentina, 1987, Mr. Apey introduced me to his friend, Angel Giminez. He was from Spain, and came to Argentina often to play and to coach. He was well known as a great tennis professional and also as a great coach. Mr. Apey felt it would be nice for Angel and me to play tennis together. He said, "Gabriela, here is my friend Angel. He has been watching you play and would like to have a game with you. What do you think?" I said, "Sure, why not." And we played. Angel was very good on the court, and we got along well.

About six months later, my father and I talked about him and his playing. We both liked him.

We also discussed that fact that he was a great coach and maybe we should consider changing. We hadn't been thinking about this before, but maybe it was time to get new experiences from a new coach. We decided to try him.

Angel Gimenez was one of my greatest coaches. He was a very hard player and worker. He developed many tennis disciplines for me to follow, such as daily tennis drills, which greatly improved my playing. His character was also very strong, and he was very serious about the game, more than anyone before.

Angel was also a very considerate coach, who understood the pressures that players had on them during the tournaments. Of all my coaches, he was the youngest, and one of the most sensitive to my needs and the needs of others. He taught me important lessons in both tennis and life, which I will never forget. We worked together for three and half years.

25

My Brother Osvaldo

I started traveling around South America for tournaments when I was ten years old. I had also been playing in tournaments in Argentina for several years. This meant leaving school at different times to compete in many foreign countries. In each place, we girls from Argentina would compete for prize money and awards against girls from other countries around the world. Except for the trip to Europe with Mercedes when I was thirteen, we generally traveled in tour groups. These were handled by the training schools. Mr. Apey arranged this for us.

By the time I was fifteen, I was becoming a better player with every match. My travel increased. I was flying to many new places every month. Sometimes, I would travel with the groups. Other times, I had to travel by myself. However, I was still too young to travel all over the world on my own. What should I do?

My big brother, Osvaldo, Jr., had the answer. Although a full time student at the university, he agreed to go with me to many of the tournaments. He's five years older than I am. This was great.

"Osvaldo," I said. "You are the best brother a girl could have. Thank you for doing this for me." Osvaldo cut back on some of his classes and went with me on many of the tours over the next year.

Later, when I was sixteen, he temporarily stopped all his classes so that he could travel with me for the whole period. This meant that he gave up all his studies, his classmates, and his girl friends. This was the greatest sacrifice, and I will never forget it. He inspired me to be generous in giving my time and attention to people and to offer them my support.

So from the time I was fourteen to seventeen, my brother traveled with me many times when I wasn't with the group. He was always there when I needed him. I don't think you could find a more giving brother anywhere.

Osvaldo gave me a lot of support. He was more than just a brother; he was also a great friend. In many ways he was like another coach, a very loving guy who was always thoughtful and thinking about how to help. He was always very kind and generous. Besides giving me his time from the university, my brother helped me to see and to understand things that I didn't really understand then. He helped to make everything clearer, and taught me so many important things about people. And if ever I was tired or down

My Brother Osvaldo

from too much travel, he lifted my spirits. I had
my strongest support from him, my number one
fan. And I'm his number one fan, too!

26

Looking for a New Coach

I needed a new coach, one who could help me to improve my tennis. He had to be able to travel with me to my tournaments. Most important of all, he should be someone whom I could like and respect. He had to be someone who would like and respect me. Dick Dell, my agent and business manager, my parents and I had been having a hard time finding just the right person. A number of people were suggested, but one name came up again and again — Carlos Kirmayr.

Carlos was a former tennis professional from South America who spoke fluent Spanish and English. He first met with Dick Dell in America, and since that meeting went well, we invited him to meet with my father and me in Argentina. When we first met him, we were not sure if he would be the right person for the job. We needed to find out if we could work together.

The relationship worked right from the start.

We all agreed that Carlos was the right coach for
me. He was very intelligent, was an excellent
teacher, and was sensitive to my tennis needs. He
really knew tennis. I don't mean just how to make
better shots, but he knew how to "think" the
game. He had a great attitude and was always
positive, not pushy or demanding the way some
coaches can be. And he made tennis fun. We
were all very happy that the relationship worked
so quickly. I liked his character very much and
that was a very important thing.

Carlos and I developed a very good working
relationship. That was something I was not
counting on at the beginning, but he was such
a warm, friendly and concerned person that he
turned out to be a great friend too. One of the
things I enjoyed most about Carlos was his
wonderful sense of humor. Here is a typical story
of what happened on our first Australian tour
together.

Carlos and I were in Australia for the
Australian Open. After our first day on the courts,
we were tired and needed to get back to our
hotel. It was late afternoon and still quite warm.
Carlos suggested that it would be fun to do something different going back to the hotel.

He said, "Let's take a pedicab. I'll bet you've
never even been on one."

I answered, "No, I never have. And what's
more, I don't know what it is."

He pointed to a thing that had three bike wheels, a seat in the front and pedals like a bicycle, and two seats side by side in the back for passengers. "It's not that far," he said, "and we'll have the fresh air to breathe. We can look at the open sky on the way."

We got in and gave the driver the name of our hotel. After tying down our tennis gear, the driver hopped on the bicycle part of the pedicab and pushed really hard to get it going. Slowly he got the speed going faster and faster until we were moving almost as fast as we could walk. We began moving into heavy traffic on the main road. This was very scary, especially since all the cars seemed to be going the wrong way. The cars drive on the left side of the road in Australia just as they do in England. We must have looked funny, since all the people were staring at us — two sweat-drenched tourists being driven this way and that, dodging traffic in the middle of the road.

The driver pedaled harder and harder. He had taken us nearly six blocks. Our hotel was only two more blocks away — and up a steep hill! The driver looked up and groaned.

"Well, here we go, mates!" he said, and began pedaling as hard as he could. We could see the sweat rolling down his back. The pedicab was going so slowly that a couple of times I thought we started slipping backwards.

I said, "Oh, you poor guy! If you like, we can just get out right here. We'll pay you the full fare."

He said, "No, that's okay. Thanks anyway, mate. I'll make it, just you wait and see."

He pedaled and puffed a little harder and made it up the hill and to our hotel. I was really impressed with the young man. He had a job to do and he would see it through no matter how hard it was.

Sometimes, when things get really tough for me, Carlos will say, "Just make believe you're a pedicab driver and push on." We laugh at the memory, and I keep pushing on.

Carlos and I had many interesting situations like that. That's one of the biggest reasons I liked Carlos so much, because he always made things funny. Even in tennis practice, he made it seem easy, like a fun game. This is sort of like what Mr. Apey did when he had us play those games in his training camp.

Carlos taught me that tennis is a game of skill and strategy. To play well a person must be very cool, and never allow negative emotions like fear, anger or worry to get in the way. You must be perfectly relaxed all the time. You must be calm, yet very alert in watching everything that is happening.

Carlos would tell me, *"Play with your heart, not with your head, and your body will follow."*

Another thing he said again and again was, *"Never ever allow yourself to get angry. The most important thing you can do during a tennis match is to keep a cool head."*

I like to live my life the way I play tennis: To love what I do, to try always to do my very best, to respect everyone I have to deal with, and always — *always!* — *to act in such a way that I will always bring the highest respect towards my family, my country, myself, and the game of tennis itself.*

27

————◆I◆————

My Special Gift

I found my career in tennis. It is my own personal and special passion and it is my own special gift.

When someone asks me, "How do I get 'into' tennis?" I say, "You must love it with all your heart because whatever you love with your heart and soul will make your life more fulfilling and enjoyable. You will do well in anything where you can use your own natural gifts."

And when people ask me "Where or how do I find my special gift like you found yours?"

I answer, "Through experience. You may not find your career in sports. Maybe it's being a lawyer, an economist or becoming a world leader. Everyone's gift is different. The key is to always keep searching for that 'special thing' or activity that you can love with all your heart, and that in which you want to do your best, that thing that gives you the most satisfaction. That thing or 'activity is your own special gift.'

I know that people have the most successful lives loving what they do and doing what it is that they do best." I truly believe that everyone is born with a special skill or gift in life. It is the real you, the most honest and the truest you. When other people see you involved in your special skills, they want to be around you, because your happiness and pride in what you are doing makes them feel good. Your success can be an example for others to follow that will help them find their own specialness.

So when you are using your special gift, you are also giving to others. And do you know what? *A giving person is the best kind of person in the world. And do you know who that person is? That person is you!!*

28

I Know That I'm Never Alone

I know when I'm out on the court facing some opponent I look as if I'm all by myself. That's just me serving or returning a serve or chasing down a volley. That's what it looks like, but the truth is, I'm not alone out there at all. I'm with everyone who has ever helped me, everyone who ever supported me, everyone who has ever cheered for me. I wouldn't even be in any of the tournaments if it hadn't been for the help I got from my parents, from Osvaldo, from Daniel Fidalgo, from Patricio Apey, from Angel Giminez, from my friend Mercedes, from Dick Dell, from Carlos Kirmayr, and maybe even the pedicab driver and the walls of my childhood! All these people and experiences are always with me. They're with me when I step onto the court and they're with me when I'm off the court. I didn't become a professional tennis player all by myself. I had help and support all the way, and that help and support has made all the difference in my success. It's the most important part of me. It's what has taught me that I too must be kind and must give a helping hand to all those who can use my help.

Appendixes

Appendix A
Career Highlights

Birth date: May 16, 1970
Birthplace: Buenos Aires, Argentina
Residence: Buenos Aires, Argentina
Plays: Righthanded
Height: 5-8
Weight: 130

1994 HIGHLIGHTS
- Semifinalist, Australian Open, Melbourne, Australia
- Finalist, Bausch & Lomb Championships, Amelia Island, FL
- Quarterfinalist, Virginia Slims of Florida, Delray Beach, FL
- Quarterfinalist, Lipton Championships, Key Biscayne, FL

1993 HIGHLIGHTS
- Finalist, Italian Open, Rome, Italy
- Finalist, Bausch & Lomb Championships, Amelia Island, FL
- Semifinalist, Virginia Slims of Los Angeles, Manhattan Beach, CA
- Semifinalist, Australian Open, Melbourne, Australia
- Semifinalist, Lipton Championships, Key

Biscayne, FL
- Semifinalist, Family Circle Cup, Hilton Head, SC
- Semifinalist, Virginia Slims of Houston, TX
- Semifinalist, N.S.W. Tournament of Champions, Sydney, Australia
- Quarterfinalist, U.S. Open, Flushing Meadows, New York
- Quarterfinalist, Wimbledon, London, England
- Quarterfinalist, French Open, Paris, France

EARLIER HIGHLIGHTS
- Champion, U.S. Open, 1990
- Champion, Lipton International Championships,1989; finalist, 1992, '91
- Champion, Virginia Slims Championships, 1988; finalist, '90; semifinalist;'92, Finalist, Wimbledon, 1991
- Winner of 25 career singles titles

WINNER - SINGLES
- 1992 - Sydney, Pan Pacific, Hilton Head. Amelia Island, Italian Open
- 1991 - Pan Pacific, Boca Raton, Hilton Head, Amelia Island, Italian Open
- 1990 - U.S. Open, Boca Raton
- 1989 - Lipton, Amelia Island, Italian Open, Filderstadt
- 1988 - Virginia Slims Championships, Boca Raton, Italian Open, Canadian Open:
- 1987 - Brighton, Pan Pacific, Argentinean Open
- 1986 - Argentinean Open
- 1985 - Japan Open

WINNER - DOUBLES
- 1990 - Canadian Open (w/Nagelson)
- 1988 - Wimbledon (w/Graf), Lipton (w/Graf)
- 1987 - Italian Open (w/Navratilova, Amelia Island (w/Graf)
- 1986 - U.S. Clay Courts (w/Graf)
- 1985 - Canadian Open (w/Garrison), European Indoors (w/Graf), Tampa (w/Bassett Seguso), Argentinean Open (w/Paz). (Junior Singles)
- 1984 - French Open, Italian Open, Orange Bowl, Banana Bowl (Junior Tournaments)
- 1983 - Banana Bowl (Junior Tournament)

FINALIST - SINGLES
- 1993 - Amelia Island, Italian Open, German Open
- 1992 - Lipton, Tokyo, Filderstadt:
- 1991 - Wimbledon, Lipton:
- 1990 - Virginia Slims Championships, European Indoors, New England
- 1989 - Los Angeles, Tampa, German Open
- 1988 - U.S. Open, Los Angeles, Hilton Head, Amelia Island, Olympics
- 1987 - Virginia Slims Championships, Italian Open
- 1986 - U.S. Clay Courts: 1985 Hilton Head, Tampa

ADDITIONAL
- Argentinean Federation Cup Team 1985-87
- Argentinean Olympic Team 1988

QUICK FACTS

- At 1993 Australian Open, three-set quarterfinal win over Mary Pierce included a 14-12 second-set tie break. Sabatini won 4-6, 7-6, 6-0
- At 1990 U.S. Open, knocked out Steffi Graf 6-2, 7-6, (7-4) in final to win first Grand Slam event in career: at same event, became lowest seed to win in 22 years (No. 5 seed), first female from Argentina to win a Grand Slam event and first South American to win U.S. Open since Brazil's Maria Bueno in 1968, by reaching 1988 U.S. Open (lost to Steffi Graf), became first female Argentinean player in history to reach a Grand Slam singles final
- Extended Monica Seles 6-4, 5-7, 3-6, 6-4, 6-2 for a first-ever five-set Virginia Slims Championship final in 1990, first women's match to go five sets since Bessie Moore beat Myrtle McAteer 6-4, 3-6, 7-5, 2-6, 6-2 at U.S. National Championships in Philadelphia in 1901
- Captured Silver Medal in singles at 1988 Olympic Games in Seoul
- Defeated Chris Evert in semifinal match at 1988 Boca Raton, first time defeat over Evert in six meetings, went on to defeat Steffi Graf in final, for first-time defeat over Graf in 12 meetings
- Won 1988 Virginia Slims Championships with wins over Katerina Maleeva, Natalie Zvereva, Helena Sukova and Pam Shriver
- Formerly youngest semifinalist ever at the

French Open; in 1985 she was 15-years and
three-weeks old when she lost to Chris Evert
in final-four; youngest now is Jennifer Capriati
(1990 French Open)
- At 1985 Hilton Head, upset three Top 10
players - Zina Garrison (No. 9), Pam Shriver
(No. 8), and Manuela Maleeva (No. 5) - to
reach final, losing to Chris Evert before a
national NBC-TV audience; jumped in the
rankings from No. 33 to No. 18 after event
- First appeared on computer at No. 72 in
October 1984
- Ranked No. 1 on ITF World Junior list for 1984;
won a total of six junior titles
- Ranked No.1 in South America and Argentina
1985-1993
- Was youngest player ever to capture the
Orange Bowl Jrs. when in 1983, she did so at
13 years, seven months and one week of age.
- In 1992, a fiery orange-red rose was named in
her honor "Gabriela Sabatini Rose" marking
the first time in history that a rose has been
named after a tennis player; other celebrity-
named roses include: Ingrid Bergman, Queen
Elizabeth, Princesse de Monaco (Grace Kelly),
Audrey Hepburn, Elizabeth Taylor, Barbara
Bush, John F. Kennedy, Bing Crosby, Picasso,
Prince Charles and Cary Grant
- The Great American Doll Company is
preparing to launch a Gaby doll

- In 1992 named to People Magazine's "50 Most Beautiful People" list
- Launched her own perfume Gabriela Sabatini in May 1989; launched second perfume Magnetic in 1992, and recently released Cascaya; all have reached best seller status in Europe
- Recipient of 1991 WTA Most Improved Player Award; named 1985 WTA Most Impressive Newcomer
- Serving second term on Special Olympics Committee (1992/93, 1993/94); named honorary chairperson of Special Olympics/WTA Players Association program in March 1993
- In 1991, signed a multi-million dollar contract with Pepsi, becoming the first female athlete to do so
- Also endorses Yamaha Racquets, Head Clothing, Fuji cameras and film, Rayban sunglasses, The Great American Doll Company, Aerolineas Argentinas and Gosen String
- Was coached by Dennis Ralston from 1993 Delray Beach through 1993 U.S. Open; working with Guillermo Vilas since mid-October 1993.
- Began playing at age 7

PERSONAL
- Father, Osvaldo, retired in 1986 after serving as a General Motors Corporation executive
- Mother's name is Beatriz
- Brother, Osvaldo Jr., born in 1965, is a good

club player and now starring on a television
show in Argentina
- Enjoys writing children's books
- Purchased full-working ranch in native
  Argentina in 1992 and appointed father as
  curator
- Helped open the first McDonald's restaurant in
  Argentina at a benefit for Children's Hospital in
  November, 1986
- Enjoys music, singing and soccer
- Likes card games and video games
- Nicknamed Gaby

Virginia Slims Ranking (Season Ending, Singles)

1993-5	1989-3	1986-10
1992-3	1988-4	1985-11
1991-3	1987-6	1984-74
1990-5		

Highest Singles Ranking: No. 3 (Feb 27, 1989-
April 1990; April 15, 1991-April 26, 1992; June 15-
August 16, 1992; September 14, 1992-Jan 31, 1993.

Appendix B
Frequently Asked Questions

Many times when I'm traveling or playing a tennis match, people will ask me questions about my personal life. Questions like: How do I practice, what foods do I eat, what are my favorite pastimes and hobbies, and others. These are all very typical. To help answer some of these questions, I have prepared the following questions with my answers.

If your question is not answered on these pages, please write it down on a piece of paper. Then mail the question, with your name, address, and telephone number to me in care of the company name at the end of this section. I love to receive letters and will write back as soon as my schedule allows.

1) *Question: What do you do on a typical day?*
Answer: This is a very good question. One of the things I like to do is to wake up early in the morning, so I can have more time to do more things during the day.

I need to sleep from nine to ten hours a night. I usually go to sleep between 11 p.m. and midnight. It is better for me to fall asleep earlier because I realized a long time ago that there's nothing better than to be well rested and to start the day with a lot of energy.

So, I usually wake up around 8:30 A.M. Then, I have a good, healthful breakfast which consists of cereal and whole wheat toast. During my breakfast, I read the newspaper, because I like to be informed about what's happening around the world. When I finish doing that, I get ready to go to my practice. I start my practice at 10:00 A.M. and usually practice two hours in the morning. I work on the things I need to improve.

Practice is something I really like to do. It is a chance to improve everyday, every moment, to know that I can get better if I want to. This might take a lot of work, but I like it. I like the feeling of giving everything I have and I like the feeling I get when I see that something I practiced and practiced is getting better and better. This is a great satisfaction. It gives me so much energy to keep working hard and it motivates me to try harder.

After practice, I go home, take a shower and have lunch. Then, I go to my bedroom and I watch some T.V. or call a friend or I listen to music. When I feel rested enough, I get up and go back to practicing again at 3:00 P.M. I practice for two more hours. By the end of the second practice session of the day, my legs will get a little tired. This is a sign for me to "push harder," by saying, "Come on! Just a few more!" This is really what counts, because when I'm in a match and I feel tired, I just have to do the same thing: Concentrate on what I have to do, push harder, and not let fatigue or little aches and pains get in the way of my goal.

Following the second practice, I go back home and have another small meal like a fruit salad. It is always important for me to eat often, but not too much. I don't need to get full, I just need enough food to give my body what it needs. Next, I do some physical training. Some days I go to the gym and other days I do some running.

And finally, I might finish at 7:30 P.M. I go home, shower, change and usually go out for dinner with my friends. Then I go to bed by 11:30 P.M. to prepare for the next great day!

2) *Question: What kind of foods do you eat?*
Answer: I like to eat very healthful foods, especially when I'm doing exercise. I feel that my body is asking for good food—nothing that has fat, like fried things or sweets—only sometimes because I love sweets! But otherwise, I eat bran things. I eat vegetables, fruits, pasta, rice, and white meat (but only two times a week).

I've read a lot of books about nutrition and they said that it is good to eat meat, but not too often. When I don't eat that much meat I feel lighter and when I'm playing tournaments, I need to have a lot of carbohydrates, because carbohydrates give me more energy. Eating carbohydrates gives me more energy and I don't feel heavy and it replaces everything I lost in the match or any workout—and I also love it!

3) *Question: Do you follow any special exercise program besides your tennis practice?*

Answer: I like to go to the gym and work out on the machines. I work mostly on my legs, to keep them strong. When I go running, sometimes I run for 45 minutes or I do sprints. I also practice certain isometric exercises. This helps me to last longer in the matches. There are many different machines and programs to improve the various muscle groups used in tennis play. These are the ones I concentrate on in my workouts.

I highly recommend exercise to everyone who is able. I feel that the best thing that could happen to a child or any person is to participate in a sport or exercise program. Your body feels good, giving you a lot of mental and physical energy. If you can make time for this, you will appreciate life and yourself even more. Exercise makes you feel good.

4) *Question: What do you feel are the best things about your career in tennis?*

Answer: Playing tennis is something I love to

do. I love the game, the challenge, the satisfaction of a victory. I love everything about it. I feel that I never stop learning. I like to see new places, to travel and meet new people. This is just wonderful. I grow so much and I learn so many things. This is a big part of my life. These are the best parts of my career.

On the other hand, nothing comes without sacrifice and work. I know I have had to make a lot of sacrifices, like leaving home, leaving my family, my friends. But it was worth it, because it gave me so many things back.

5) *Question: Do you recommend tennis or sports as a career for everyone?*

Answer: As I've explained in this book, tennis is my passion, my love. This is what I chose to do, play tennis. Every person has to choose what he or she likes to do. When I started I didn't know that I was going to be a good tennis player, it was just what I wanted to do and to have fun. Each person must search for their own love, their own special gift. And we all have one. I cannot recommend tennis or any other career to anyone, because I am not them.

6) *Question: Do you like traveling? What do you do for fun in these different countries?*

Answer: When I first started to travel, it was one of the things that I liked the least. I always

liked my country, Argentina, very much. I also
had my family and friends there, and at that time
they couldn't travel with me that much. So it was
a little bit hard. As the years went by, I started to
enjoy this part more and more. I guess this was
because as I got older, I realized that there are
more things besides tennis to enjoy. Today I love
to travel, to see different places, and to meet
people. I think I'm a very lucky person, because
I have the opportunity to travel all over the world.
Sometimes it is hard to visit places, because I
have to play or practice. If I have a really busy
match schedule, I can only go out at night, maybe
for dinner or a play. This is because I have to go
to sleep early for the next day on the courts.
I find it a little boring to be on long flights. For
example, when I go to Tokyo, I try to sleep, but
I find it very hard. If I don't sleep, I write or read
or watch movies or listen to music.

7) *Question: Do you have any hobbies or pastimes?*
Answer: I love music. I like to listen, I love to
sing or write songs. After I've written a song, I
love to sing it. And this is one of the things that
helps me the most to learn English. When I
started to spend more time in the United States,
I didn't know a word of English and I knew
it was necessary for me to learn it. I have
always had people around me who spoke

English—the wife of my coach, for example;
I used to ask her if I didn't understand a word,
so I was asking all the time. I found this a great
combination. I loved music and I needed to learn
English so it really helped me a lot.

Another thing I like to do when I'm on the
road traveling is to write. I think it is a good idea
to write, for different reasons. First, because I
love to do it. Second, because sometimes I don't
have anyone to talk to at that moment and I can
do it by writing. And third, it helps me in the
future. For example I can go back and read what
I was feeling at that moment.

I also like to go shopping and buy clothes.
I also like to do some sightseeing, and visit
different places in each city. Of course, this only
happens when I have the time. I like to go out
for dinner with friends. I usually go to Italian
or Japanese restaurants; those are my favorite
places.

I love to spend time with my friends. This
could be on the road or at home. Fortunately, I
have friends on the tennis circuit, in all the countries where I play. I believe that the most important thing in life is to be surrounded by people
you care for, people you love. It is great to share
things with them. That is a reason to be happy.

8) *Question: Please tell me a little about your
family.*

Answer: We have always been very close to each other. My family has been very supportive of me throughout my personal and professional life. I don't think I would be where I am without them. My family is very important to me. They showed me how to be a good person, to enjoy life, to live every moment, to be honest.

They never told me, "You must do that" or, "You must do this." I always did what I chose to do. When you're little, you need your parents to decide for you, because you still don't know much about things, what's better or worse. They are the people who are going to care more about you in your whole life than anyone else. Once you start growing up, you start to understand life. Then you begin searching for your own independence. This is when you feel you can start making your own decisions. When this started to happen to me, I felt good about it. It was nice to grow up, but I always liked my parents' opinions. I felt comfortable with them and trusted their opinions on many different things. This helped me a lot, and helped guide me to my own independence. Today I can make my own decisions, but I always hear and value their opinions, whether I agree with them or not.

My big brother, Osvaldo, is five years older than me. He is now an actor. He started to act in 1993 and he's enjoying it very much. Now we have two famous members in the family. I have a very good relationship with my brother. He is a great guy and very supportive of me. I really adore him. When we were little we used to fight all the time. My parents would get so mad but we always used to play games together. I remember we had a big terrace at home and we used to play tennis on it. We would put chairs in the middle of the terrace, piled on top of each other and pretend it was the net. We would spend hours out there, but at the end of course, we would start to fight. So I started to play tennis because of him. I used to follow my brother in all the things he would do. He was the one who first started to play tennis seriously.

Appendix C
Lessons for Life

———————◗◖———————

I have learned many valuable lessons in the course of my professional career. Some were learned through my own efforts and experiences (see my three "Lessons for Life"). Other lessons were learned from the examples of others. One strong example is that of my brother, Osvaldo. Do you remember that he traveled with me on my international tours? He postponed his university studies for three years to do this. It was his idea, his feeling, and he did it because he knew it would help me. It was because of his help that I could do and learn so much in my career. Osvaldo has since returned to school, graduated, and is now a popular actor on national television in Argentina. I'm so very proud of him.

LEARNING FROM OTHERS: I learned a very valuable "Lesson for Life" from Osvaldo: To do things for others is to do good things for yourself. I learned to be considerate and helpful towards other people whenever and wherever I could. That is the lesson that I would like to share with you now.

SPECIAL EXERCISE PLAN: To help you feel what I felt, I have made a special exercise plan. This plan is made up of two exercises. Both exercises can be practiced on different days in any order whenever you want to do them. When successfully completed, you will have experienced the joys of sharing good thoughts, feelings, and deeds with others. You will learn that the more things you do for others, the more you really do for yourself, and the more you will like yourself and other people.

SPECIAL CERTIFICATE OF COMPLETION: Follow the instructions at the end of the exercises. When you complete the lesson, you will receive a *Certificate of Completion* signed by me which will be mailed to you. This certificate is very beautiful and is suitable for framing on your wall. Share in my world and experience your own good feelings by following these easy and fun exercises today. I want you to make this *your very own "Lesson for Life."*

Lesson Number 1

Doing Things for Others

(PLEASE PRINT)

Your name: _Amy Jay Wiley_

Street address: _12610 NE 37th Ct_

City: _Vancouver_

State: _Washington_ Zip: _98686_

Date of birth: _September 21, 1993_

EXERCISE ONE
Learning to Say Nice Things

Today's date is 12\30\03

On this first exercise you will learn to say something nice to another person. Think about who is one of the people you like most in the world.

1. After you have chosen that person, write the person's name here:

2. Write one thing you really like about this person.

3. When you next see this person tell her/him what you have written. Write, in the following

spaces, what you told that person.

I told (person's name)_____

on (date)___January 5, 2004_____

that I liked:_____

in class (not)_____

_____

_____

_____

_____

_____

_____

_____ about her/him.

4. Write what happened when you told this person

(person's name)_____

what you liked best about her/him. Describe the
reaction. Was she/he pleased? Did she/he smile?

_____

_____

_____

_____

_____

_____

_____

5. Write below how you felt when you told this
person what you liked about her/him.

I Felt kinda embarrased.
                                      (not)

_____

_____

_____

_____

_____

I (your name) _Amy_____

have completed *Exercise One* from the Gabriela
Sabatini "Doing Things for Others," Lesson One.

My signature

_Amy Wiley_____

My parent's or guardian's signature

_____

Exercise Two
Doing Something Nice for Someone in My Family

Your name: _Amy Jay Wiley_

Today's date is _12\30\03_

Now you are going to plan to do something nice for someone. The person you choose may be anyone in your family, **but she/he must live with you!** This is very important. Think of a person in your family whom you know very well and for whom you would like to do something special. Here are a few examples to help you get started. You can select any one of these, or you can make up your own thoughtful deeds. Whatever you choose, be sure the person you are doing this for will be VERY HAPPY when she/he sees what you have done. **Example One—Your Mother or Father is the person you have chosen.**

You may decide to: Set the table for dinner; surprise your mom with some flowers; clean out a closet; take out the trash; or write a special letter to that person about how much you like her/him, and why. Or, perhaps you know something that is even better than any of the ideas listed here. You can do anything you like, and make it fun.

1. The person in my family I chose is:

_____

This person is my _____

(write if this is your mother, father, grandparent, sister, brother, or someone else you like.)

2. This is what I did: _____

_____

_____

_____

_____

_____

_____

3. Describe below what the person's reaction was when you did this special thing:

_____

_____

_____

_____

_____

_____

_____

4. Describe how the person in your family felt
when you did something special for her/him:

_____

_____

_____

_____

_____

_____

_____

_____

5. Write below how you felt when you did your
nice thing for this person.

_____

_____

_____

_____

_____

_____

I (your name)_____
have completed *Exercise Two* from the Gabriela
Sabatini "Doing Things for Others" Lesson.

My signature

_____

My parent's or guardian's signature

_____

When you have finished both exercises, mail them to me to receive your own **"Certificate of Completion"** (see directions below.) This certificate will certify that you have successfully completed two exercises in Gaby's "Lessons for Life" Book One.

DIRECTIONS: To receive your own Certificate of Completion, mail the two completed exercises, with your name and address, and $2.00 to cover processing and postage, to:

GABRIELA SABATINI
C/O **GREAT AMERICAN PUBLICATIONS**
438 East Katella Avenue
Department 226
Orange, California 92667

If you enjoyed reading Gabriela Sabatini's real life stories and working through her important Lessons for Life™ and would like to read more, you can write to her by filling out the form on the next page. Please send it to:

GABRIELA SABATINI
C/O GREAT AMERICAN PUBLICATIONS
438 East Katella Avenue
Department 226
Orange, California 92667

Dear Gabriela,

I would love to read more of your real life stories. Please send me information about your next book and when it will become available. Also, please include my name on your mailing list for notification of future publications. Thank you.

My name is:

_____

I live at (address):

_____

City:_____

State:_____ Zip:_____

My Parent's signature:

_____

(Please answer the following questions.)

1. How did you find out about this book?

_____

2. What did you like the most about this book?

_____

_____

_____